11/22
2

39.60

TEEN LIFE™

FREQUENTLY ASKED QUESTIONS ABOUT

Smoking

Veronica Stollers
and
Elizabeth Keyishian

ROSEN
PUBLISHING®

New York

Published in 2012 by The Rosen Publishing Group, Inc.
29 East 21st Street, New York, NY 10010

First Edition

Library of Congress Cataloging-in-Publication Data

Stollers, Veronica.
Frequently asked questions about smoking / Veronica Stollers,
Elizabeth Keyishian.
    p. cm.—(FAQ: Teen life)
Includes bibliographical references and index.
ISBN 978-1-4488-4631-3 (library binding)
1. Youth—Tobacco use—Juvenile literature. 2. Smoking—
Juvenile literature. 3. Nicotine addiction—Juvenile literature.
I. Keyishian, Elizabeth. II. Title.
HV5745.S736 2012
613.85—dc22

                                        2010048419

Manufactured in the United States of America

CPSIA Compliance Information: Batch #S11YA: For further information, contact Rosen Publishing, New York, New York,
at 1-800-237-9932.

Contents

WHY DO PEOPLE START SMOKING?

According to the Centers for Disease Control and Prevention (CDC), about 20 percent of high school students smoke, while a little over 6 percent of middle school students smoke. Each day, about 3,900 young people between the ages of 11 and 17 try their first cigarette. Almost 950 of these teens will become daily smokers. If you ask these teens if they think they will still be smoking in five years, 97 percent of them will say no. They are wrong. According to the American Cancer Society (ACS), studies have found that 60 percent of them will still be smokers seven to nine years later. Most teen smokers report that they would love to quit but are unable to do so. Although the rate of teen smokers is down from recent years, it is still staggering to think that half of these new smokers will ultimately die as a result of their smoking habit.

Many teens don't realize that just trying one cigarette can lead to a lifetime of addiction. According to the American Cancer Society, nearly all first-time use of tobacco occurs before high school graduation.

Many people, especially teens, want to be cool, fit in, and have friends. However, picking up a harmful, potentially lifelong habit does not make a person cool. What also isn't cool is that smoking causes death. The American Lung Association (ALA) states that smoking kills nearly four hundred thousand Americans each year. It kills about thirty-seven thousand Canadians each year. According to the Lung Association, the average smoker will die eight years earlier than his or her nonsmoking counterpart.

Selling Smoking

So, how is it that everyone seems to know how bad cigarettes are for you, and yet people still start smoking? Well, smoking addiction is big business for tobacco companies. The entire tobacco industry is a multibillion-dollar business. Each year, more than one million smokers successfully quit. Tobacco companies must use advertising to attract new smokers. They target young adults, especially teens, because they are just starting to make choices about their lives. Clever yet deceptive advertising makes smoking seem like a lifestyle choice that is fun, rewarding, and socially acceptable. According to the ALA, the tobacco industry spent more than $12.49 billion on advertising in 2006. That is a lot of money being spent to get you interested in a deadly habit.

Cigarette advertisements do not tell the whole story. Tobacco companies are now paying a price for not revealing the health risks associated with smoking. Across the country, they are being sued for millions of dollars by smokers with smoking-related health problems and by the families of people who have died from smoking-related illnesses. Many cases are settled out of court. This means that tobacco companies give money to the smokers and smokers' families so that the cases do not go to court. This prevents tobacco companies from getting bad publicity. It also keeps all the facts about smoking and related health problems from being easily known.

Cigarette advertisers have a hard task to do. They must create ads that make smoking seem like a great thing. Smoking has to look good enough for you to want to try it, even though the ad, by law, has to warn you that smoking is harmful. This law was passed so that everyone would know the dangers of smoking.

Older people who smoke do not need advertising to convince them. A lot of people who smoke would stop if they could, but they are hooked. Smoking is a habit. Many people become addicted to the nicotine in tobacco. Their bodies need it, and they feel sick or nervous if they do not smoke.

Most adults who don't smoke will not be swayed into smoking by cigarette ads. At their age, they probably already know the truth. This is why tobacco companies target younger audiences. They want to reach the easy sale, or the customer who doesn't yet know the dangers of smoking. They want to reach young people who are beginning to define themselves. Young people experiment and search for different ways of expressing themselves. Tobacco companies' advertisements want to tell you that you'll be cool if you smoke.

Cigarette ads make it look as if you will have fun because you smoke. They make you think that smoking will make you popular. That kind of advertising suggestion is called association. Association means linking one idea with another. Cigarette ads try to link pleasant things with their product.

Often the ads show people outdoors playing sports. In real life, people who smoke a lot can have trouble breathing. Smoking makes it hard to play active sports. If you are on a team, the coach will tell you not to smoke.

Cigarette ads show people who are healthy, with glowing skin and brilliant white teeth. In truth, smoking stains your teeth. It makes your skin dull, and it makes your hair smell bad.

Advertising and Young People

Although it is against the law to sell cigarettes to minors (people younger than eighteen), cigarette ads seem to be directed toward younger and younger kids. According to a study conducted by the ALA, more than 30 percent of teens began smoking because of a tobacco company's advertising activities. Fortunately, there are government agencies and private organizations that are fighting to protect teens from this kind of advertising trick. Back in 1996, the U.S. Food and Drug Administration (FDA) issued regulations to limit the advertising of cigarettes and smoking to young people. These regulations included a ban on tobacco billboards within 1,000 feet (305 meters) of schools and playgrounds. Many people think that cigarette advertising should not be allowed. It is no longer allowed on television. In New York City, cigarette advertising is no longer allowed on buses or subways.

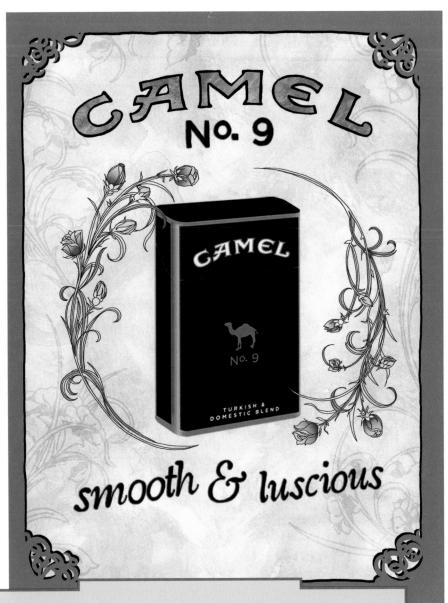

Fashion-themed cigarette advertisements like this one specifically target young women. When this ad came out in 2007, surveys showed that the number of young women who cited Camel as their favorite brand of cigarettes sharply increased.

Some companies have even used cartoon characters to advertise cigarettes. A classic and still well-known example is Joe Camel. In 1997, the R. J. Reynolds Tobacco Company retired its cartoon character, Joe Camel. A 1991 study in the *Journal of the American Medical Association* showed that children were as aware of the image of Joe Camel as they were of Fred Flintstone or Mickey Mouse. The study showed that children as young as three years old knew who Joe Camel was and that he was associated with cigarettes. In November 1998, the outcome of a multistate settlement with the tobacco industry banned the use of cartoon characters for tobacco advertising. This means that the tobacco industry agreed to stop using characters like Joe Camel to sell its products. But these restrictions don't necessarily mean that tobacco companies have stopped targeting young people. A study published in *Pediatrics* in March 2010 found that Camel No. 9 cigarettes, targeted at women, were attracting the attention of teenage girls. Ads showing a shiny black box and hot pink accents ran in magazines like *Cosmopolitan* and *Vogue*, and promotional items like lip balm, purses, and cell phone jewelry were used in the marketing. R. J. Reynolds denied claims that it was targeting teenage girls, but the study argues that whether or not teens were targeted directly, the ads still hit their mark and captured the attention of girls.

Cigarette makers would never publicly reveal the hazards of cigarette smoking, since they would lose huge amounts of money. Lawsuits against tobacco companies are common across the United States. In March 1999, a jury in Oregon ordered the tobacco company Philip Morris to pay $81 million to the family of a man

Shira Yevin, seen here, is speaking for the American Legacy Foundation's "truth" campaign, which spreads the message about the dangers of smoking. A recent study shows that campaigns like this one help increase the decline of youth smoking.

who smoked Marlboro cigarettes for forty years before he died. In a 2010 case in Florida, a woman was awarded $10.8 million after her husband passed away because of a lifetime of smoking.

Advertising Against Smoking

There is another side to more recent cigarette advertising. Health-related groups like the American Cancer Society and the American Heart Association (AHA) have ads, too. Their ads warn of the dangers of smoking. Getting out the message about the dangers of smoking is very important. The cigarette companies spend more than $12 billion a year to convince people that smoking is not bad for them. Now there is something being done to let people know the truth about smoking. Organizations like Truth are able to get through to young people because they employ eye-catching commercials and try to be provocative in their message. These groups are utilizing social networking and interactive contests to engage young people.

Some cigarette companies spend money advertising against teen smoking. It would seem counter to the tobacco companies' goals, but some studies show that advertising, such as Lorillard Tobacco Company's "Tobacco Is Whacko If You're a Teen" campaign, can actually make smoking more appealing to teenagers.

chapter two

WHAT ARE THE HEALTH RISKS OF SMOKING?

We know that tobacco companies work very hard to make smoking seem attractive, but you don't listen to every ad you see, so why exactly do most people start smoking? Many young people start smoking because other people around them do. Their parents, brothers and sisters, relatives, or friends smoke, so it does not seem like a big deal. You may even think that you should smoke because others do and you want to be like them. Fortunately, we can admire someone without picking up his or her bad habits. You can still admire the smokers in your life, even while knowing that smoking is a dead end.

The media sometimes shows us that smoking is a sign of freedom, rebellion, or being fashionable. An action

This woman is protesting outside the office of the Motion Picture Association of America. She is encouraging the association to stop showing smoking in movies targeted at children.

hero in a movie may light up a cigarette after getting the bad guys. A high-powered and stressed-out financial whiz may take a long drag on a cigarette during a deal.

Smoking does not appear to be dangerous because so many people seem to be doing it, and there do not seem to be any negative side effects. Fortunately, many states have restrictions about cigarette promotion and use in the media. Also, the theatrical industry has made attempts to limit the use of cigarettes as props in recent years.

Even though smoking may be presented as a casual choice, it is really a big deal. The nicotine in cigarettes has been found to be more addictive than crack cocaine or alcohol. The younger you are when you start, the harder it is to quit as an adult. In other words, you may think that you can smoke a cigarette here and there in social situations, and that's it. It is not that simple, however.

Without even knowing it, you can become addicted to smoking just by having an occasional cigarette. After smoking a few cigarettes, your body starts to crave nicotine. In one study, 90 percent of young people who tried to stop smoking experienced withdrawal symptoms. Withdrawal symptoms are signs that the body still craves something. In this case, it's nicotine. These are some withdrawal symptoms of smoking.

- Dry mouth
- Sore throat, gums, or tongue
- Coughing
- Headaches

- Sleeping troubles
- Irregularity (not going to the bathroom on a regular basis)
- Fatigue
- Hunger
- Tenseness, irritability

Remember, smoking is not something that you have to do. If you never do it, you will never miss it, and you will never experience the struggle of addiction. Smoking is not something that you would naturally do, like eating or sleeping. So why even start?

Think about it: smoking is not healthy because it causes illness. Smoking-related illnesses and problems include the following:

- Lung cancer and other smoking-related cancers
- Heart disease
- Stained teeth and bad breath
- Respiratory problems, such as coughing and wheezing
- Loss of the ability to smell and taste
- Infertility problems in women

Still, it might be hard if you have friends who start smoking and want you to try it, too. You may feel pressure to light up with your friends so that you can fit in and be part of the group. The main thing to remember, though, is that your body is yours and no one else's. You will suffer the consequences of what smoking does to your body, and you will also be hurting people around you with the secondhand smoke of cigarettes. Secondhand

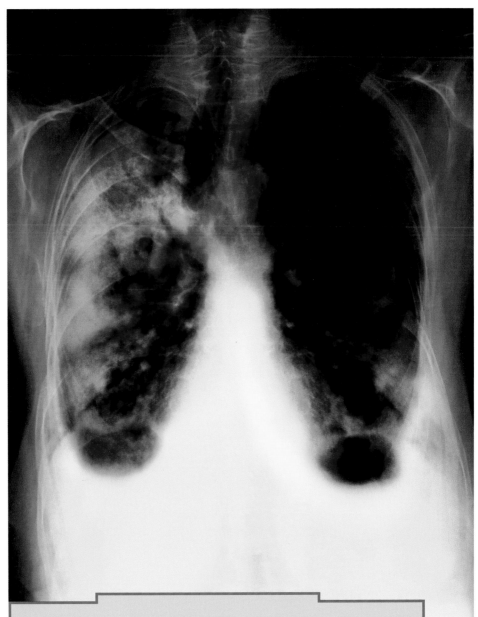

Smoking causes tar to build up in the lungs, which can cause infections and make breathing difficult. This X-ray shows a pair of unhealthy human lungs.

smoke is the smoke that fills the air from a lit cigarette and a smoker's lungs. It is your choice whether to smoke, but know that smoking is not an easy habit to end. You will find that standing up to peer pressure is much easier than standing up to nicotine dependence.

It can get confusing when you see adults smoke. You may wonder why someone grown up would make a choice like smoking if it is wrong. You may even start smoking so that you can feel like an adult. Chances are, if you asked any adult smokers, they'd tell you not to do it. These adults are using a substance that has a powerful addiction cycle. Besides, it doesn't make you seem older, but it does age your skin. This means wrinkles and saggy skin. If you want to feel like a grown-up, make good choices about your health.

You can tell that smoking is bad for you by the way your body reacts to it. The first time you smoke, it usually makes you cough. You may choke or feel dizzy. You may even feel sick enough to throw up. Cigarette smoke contains tar, which stays in your lungs even though you blow the smoke back out through your nose or mouth. Tar in your lungs can cause cancer. Smoking can also cause heart disease and other serious health problems. Even if you do enjoy smoking, is the pleasure worth sacrificing your health or even your life?

Smoking and Cancer

We have learned that smoking can lead to heart disease and lung cancer. The National Institutes of Health (NIH) found that 87 percent of all lung cancer deaths are linked to smoking. Not only that, but according to the ACS, lung cancer is currently the leading cause of cancer death in the United States for both men and women. Smoking doesn't just cause lung cancer. It is linked to a number of different cancers as well. In fact, tobacco use accounts for at least 30 percent of all cancer deaths. A study reported that there is even a link between cigarette smoking and colon cancer. If you start smoking when you are young, the increased risk of colon cancer stays with you even after you quit. In other words, smoking can cause permanent damage. Other cancers associated with smoking are the following:

- Mouth
- Pharynx
- Larynx
- Esophagus
- Stomach
- Pancreas
- Cervix
- Kidney
- Bladder

It may not seem important now, but your body and its health are important. Your body must be able to last through your young and middle years to a healthy old age. Many adults try to improve the health of their bodies so that they can live longer. You may probably become one of these adults, so why not get a head start? Why not try to avoid certain diseases that are linked to smoking?

What Exactly Is Inside That Cigarette and What Is It Doing to Lungs?

To understand how terrible smoking is for you, look at what each cigarette contains:

- Nicotine, a habit-forming drug.
- Black tars that stick to the lining of your lungs and make it hard to breathe.
- Chemicals that poison your body. These chemicals include arsenic, carbon monoxide, nitrogen oxide, cyanide, formaldehyde, lead, and ammonia.
- DDT, which is an insecticide (a poison for killing insects).

Every drag on a cigarette leaves those things in your lungs. In addition, nicotine speeds up your heart and makes you feel shaky. You quickly become addicted to it.

Tars coat the inside of your lungs and make it hard to breath. Your heart has to work harder. It is not getting enough oxygen from your stuffed-up lungs. Carbon monoxide prevents oxygen from reaching your heart. That can cause heart disease.

Your body is a sensitive machine. The various parts of the body work together to keep you healthy. When you smoke, you damage many parts of the machine, which makes it break down. Soon the machine stops working.

Simple tasks, like running up a flight of stairs, become much more difficult for a smoker. A smoker's body has more trouble adjusting to the increased demands caused by exercise.

According to the ALA, each of us breathes about 3,400 gallons of air each day. You breathe all day long. You take about 600 million breaths during your lifetime. It's easy to take breathing for granted. When was the last time you noticed that you were breathing? You probably have too many other things to think about. You think about breathing only when it hurts or becomes hard to breathe. Smoking will change breathing from a natural, unnoticeable activity to a difficult experience.

Try running up a flight of stairs. Your breathing increases to allow your lungs to take in more oxygen. Your heart rate increases. Your body naturally and easily adjusts to the increased demands on it (the increased demand is running). A smoker does not have it so easy.

The ingredients from smoking that are left behind in the body make natural activities harder. It is harder for the body to adjust to increased demands. There are pictures that can show you what happens to your lungs and heart when you smoke. Surgeons who operate on smokers say that the lungs are black from tar instead of the normal, healthy pink.

Smoking's Assault on Life Processes

The lungs bring oxygen into the body and pump carbon dioxide out. Two tubes called bronchi lead to the lungs. Branches of the tubes lead into tiny balloon-like sacs. Tiny hairs brush mucus out of the airways. These hairs are called cilia.

Nicotine, the drug in tobacco, paralyzes your cilia. According to the Lung Association, even one cigarette can slow down the

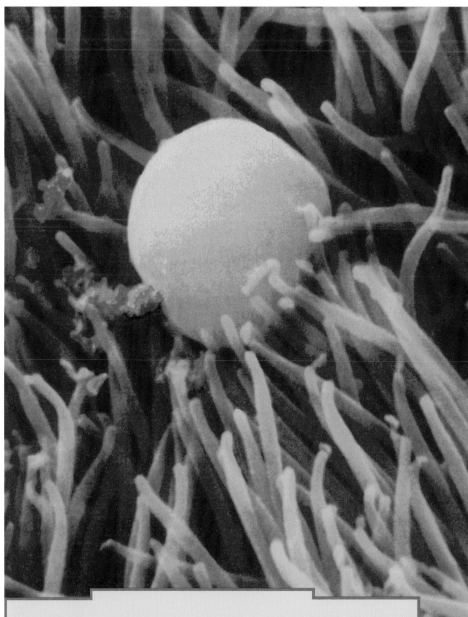

This magnified image shows what cilia in the trachea look like as they remove mucus *(the yellow sphere)* from airways. Smoking damages the cilia, making it difficult for them to do this important job.

cilia, preventing them from working properly. Large amounts of smoke kill the cilia. The cilia cannot push the mucus out of the way, so your airways get clogged. Tars and chemicals settle in the airways, and the cilia die. The smoker has to cough to get the mucus out of the lungs. That is known as smoker's cough. It sounds as if the person is choking and wheezing. The bronchi get sore with all that coughing. The smoker then develops chronic bronchitis. It becomes more painful and difficult to breathe.

People with bronchitis often develop emphysema. This is a disease that makes it hard to breathe. Many of these people have to use a wheelchair. Simple movements, like walking and breathing, become hard to perform. You may have seen someone with emphysema. People with emphysema often take a cart carrying a heavy tank of oxygen wherever they go. Just think, the people who developed emphysema from smoking went from carrying around one little cigarette to carrying around a device that helps them breathe. That's a big change, and it all starts with the choice to start smoking.

People who smoke for a long time may also get cancer. Chemicals from smoking affect the cells of the body. They can cause the cells to grow abnormally or out of control. The cells form lumps, or tumors. Not all tumors are cancerous. Smoking does, however, cause cells to become cancerous. The tumors that form because of smoking are cancerous. These tumors block breathing. The cancer may even spread to other parts of the body.

Fortunately, your body may be able to fight the effects of smoking once you have stopped. The body begins to repair itself. The body begins to rebuild damaged cells. It slowly cleanses the lungs that are black and damaged from smoking. Eventually, the body may return to a healthy state.

The Additional Risks to Women's Health

Smoking is dangerous for everybody, but there are special health risks for women. According to the ALA, although there has been a decline in smoking among high school girls, the rate of the decline is shrinking. Between 1999 and 2003, smoking among high school girls declined by 37 percent, whereas between 2003 and 2007, the decrease was only 15 percent. That might be due to cigarette advertising. It may also be because they think that cigarettes help keep their weight down. This is not true, however.

Smoking may make people feel less hungry. Many smokers believe that it provides something to do besides snack. While you may be keeping your hands and mouth busy with smoking, you're damaging your body. A person thinks that she is losing weight, but what's really happening is her health is being ruined. There are many other ways to lower or maintain your weight. You can still eat snacks, just pick something healthy, such as fruit. Sports and exercise are fun ways to spend time with friends, and these activities keep your body strong and healthy. They are also other ways to maintain your weight.

Lung cancer has replaced breast cancer as the leading killer disease of women, though more women are diagnosed with breast cancer than with lung cancer. If you smoke and take birth control pills, you are ten times more likely to have a heart attack

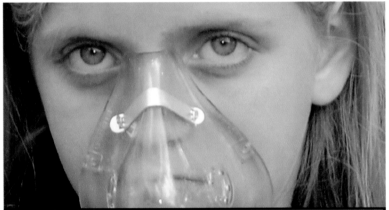

The Food and Drug Administration requires cigarette companies to put warnings on all tobacco products so that people will know the dangers cigarettes pose not only to themselves, but also to those around them.

or stroke. As you age, especially if you're over thirty-five, these risks increase. Smoking increases the risk of heart attack for young women more than any other factor. You do not have to be old to have a heart attack.

Remember the warning label on cigarette packaging: "Smoking by pregnant women may result in fetal injury, premature birth, and low birth weight." Why should you worry about that now? It may not seem important to you yet, but once you start smoking, it is very, very hard to quit. When you become a mother, you may still be smoking.

Babies of mothers who smoke have twice the risk of sudden infant death syndrome (SIDS). This disease kills babies suddenly in their sleep. Also, the babies of smokers have twice as many lung illnesses, such as bronchitis and pneumonia.

three

WHAT IS NICOTINE?

Every day we hear about the horrors of drug addiction. We read in the news about people overdosing on heroin or killing somebody to get money for crack. These are extreme cases of addiction, and most of us wouldn't guess that cigarettes are in the same category.

Like alcohol, nicotine is a legal drug. That does not make it any less of a drug, however. It may not have the immediate drastic effects of heroin or crack, but like those drugs, it is addictive. Smokers crave nicotine. They continue to smoke even though they know that it is harming them. Smokers often go through withdrawal and relapse after quitting. These things characterize drug addiction.

Cigarettes are addictive because they contain nicotine. Nicotine is a powerful and addictive drug. It is also a poison. A large amount of nicotine injected directly into the bloodstream could kill a human in less than an hour.

Nicotine is what gives smokers a "buzz," or a high, when they smoke. It is what hooks smokers and keeps them coming back for more. Even if someone successfully quits, it is not uncommon for him or her to start smoking again as much as a year or more after the last cigarette.

When Nicotine Takes Hold

Nicotine levels range from high to low in a person's bloodstream. A low nicotine level means that there isn't a great deal of nicotine circulating through the bloodstream. When the nicotine level in the bloodstream gets low, the body signals the mind: "Smoke a cigarette. I need nicotine." As soon as the smoker lights up, the nicotine is drawn into the lungs. From the lungs, it is quickly absorbed into the bloodstream. The body's nicotine craving is satisfied, for a while.

When inhaled, nicotine travels very quickly from the cigarette to the brain. Nicotine very quickly:

- Contracts the blood vessels, which lowers the temperature in the feet and hands
- Increases blood pressure
- Increases the heart rate
- Makes muscles relax

Nicotine is a sneaky drug. When you first start smoking, you will find that it gives you a little burst of energy. That is the nicotine speeding up your heart. After a while, you will notice that

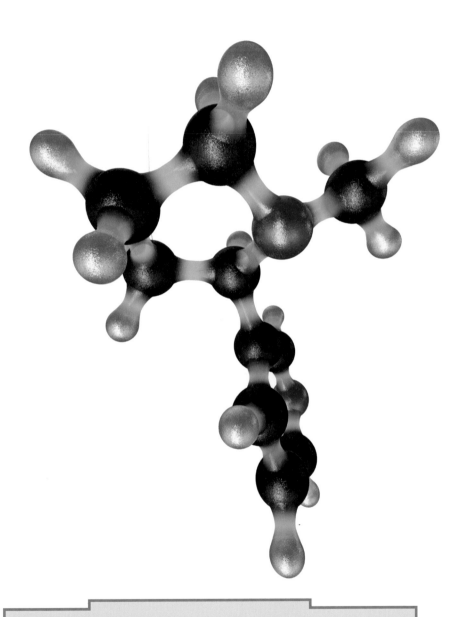

Millions of molecules just like this one make up the substance nicotine. Nicotine is a colorless, transparent liquid that is intensely poisonous.

you feel tired between cigarettes. That happens when the nicotine level gets low. The tired feeling is your body's way of telling you that it wants nicotine.

The smoker is stuck in a drug cycle. It's as if he or she is stuck on a seesaw. When "down" on the seesaw, the body feels withdrawal. That is what makes the smoker feel tired and sluggish. The body wants its dose of nicotine.

When a cigarette is smoked, the body goes "up" on the seesaw. Nicotine speeds up the heart, and it gives you a rush. It stimulates the adrenal gland. That is the gland that makes

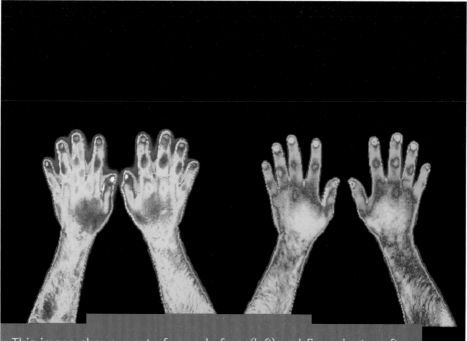

This image shows a set of arms before *(left)* and five minutes after *(right)* smoking a cigarette. The arms of the person who has just smoked are cooler because the reaction from the nicotine has caused the veins to constrict so that less blood can flow through them.

adrenaline. Adrenaline is the stuff that pumps through our veins when we are excited or nervous. Nicotine gives the same kind of rush, but when its level goes down, withdrawal symptoms kick in. So, although some people smoke to wake themselves up, they end up being more tired.

Alternatives to Nicotine

The main reason it is so difficult to quit smoking is nicotine addiction. In addition to this, several other factors make quitting a challenge. For one thing, smoking is a habit. Habits are hard to break. A smoker may also feel that smoking helps keep her weight down or ease her stress. Any one of these reasons can make quitting difficult.

Many people smoke to relieve the normal stress of everyday life. This isn't a good long-term solution. Long-term health problems such as lung cancer and heart disease aren't a good payoff for easing day-to-day stress. Nothing in your daily life is worth getting lung cancer or heart disease. Some teens might seek comfort in cigarettes. However, it is much better to talk to someone about your problems, such as a teacher, counselor, friend, nurse, or doctor. These people can offer support and helpful advice better than a pack of cigarettes can.

Instead of turning to nicotine to calm down, smokers could try

- Relaxing with a good book
- Taking a nap
- Watching a movie

Soaking in a bubble bath

Having dinner or lunch with a good friend

A way to deal with stress without cigarettes is to get energized. Finding hobbies or projects, dancing around the room to music, going for a run, or even yelling into a pillow are all healthy ways to deal with stress without smoking.

If you anticipate a stressful situation coming up, such as a test or a big game, plan ahead. Take extra time for your healthy stress busters. Do not try to relieve your stress with something like smoking, which will only cause you harm.

Ten Great Questions to Ask Your Doctor

1 How long will it take for the urge to smoke to go away after I quit?

2 How can I stop the cravings?

3 Can you tell me about how the nicotine patch works?

4 Is there a smoking cessation medication that I can take?

5 How can I keep from gaining weight as I quit smoking?

6 What are the symptoms that I will experience as I go through withdrawal?

7 I have tried to quit before but was unsuccessful. What can I do to make this time different?

8 How long does nicotine stay in the body?

9 How does smoking tobacco affect my asthma?

10 What kinds of activities can I do to avoid smoking?

four

WHAT IS SECOND-HAND SMOKE?

You may have heard this expression before: "Kissing a smoker is like licking an ashtray." Smoker's breath has also been called zoo breath. And smelly breath isn't the only drag about a smoker. That cloud of smoke you see settles in the hair and clothes, too. Smoking also causes teeth to turn yellow or gray. It causes brown or yellow marks on the fingers as well.

Not smoking saves people around you. Secondhand smoke is the smoke that you see leaving a smoker's mouth. It is also the smoke that burns from a lit cigarette. There are more than four thousand chemicals, many of them harmful, in this smoke.

Some smokers make a point to blow it away from the people standing nearby them. This doesn't stop the smoke from being harmful. The health risks that the smoker faces are the same for someone who is breathing in the

The smoke emitted directly from a lit cigarette is more dangerous than the smoke that has been exhaled by a smoker. This type of secondhand smoke is called sidestream smoke.

smoke. Secondhand smoke causes cancer. According to the National Cancer Institute (NCI), it causes 3,400 lung cancer deaths in the United States each year. It also causes forty-six thousand heart-related deaths each year. Secondhand smoke is also known as environmental tobacco smoke.

If your friends smoke, think about how it may be harming you. Many nonsmokers believe that smoking is disgusting. Some even think that it is a sign of weakness. Smokers may be limiting the types of friends they can have. If you smoked, you would be hanging out with other smokers or with people who wouldn't care if your smoke was harming them.

Breaking Down Secondhand Smoke

There are two kinds of secondhand smoke:

- Mainstream smoke
- Sidestream smoke

Mainstream smoke is what the smoker inhales into his or her lungs and then releases into the air. Think of a smoker taking a drag in slow motion. The smoke passes through the filter of the cigarette. The filter traps some of the chemicals and tars. Then the smoke enters the lungs. The lungs filter out more of the harmful substances. Finally, the smoker exhales.

Sidestream smoke is the smoke that goes directly into the air from the tip of a burning cigarette. While this smoke may seem less harmless than mainstream, it actually isn't. According to the

A woman sits before twelve thousand shoes at a rally against smoking. These shoes represent the number of people who die every year from tobacco use and secondhand smoke.

Lung Association, studies have shown that sidestream smoke contains many more chemicals than mainstream smoke. Because it does not pass through a filter, it contains a lot more carbon monoxide, tar, and nicotine than mainstream smoke. The study also found that about 85 percent of secondhand smoke is sidestream smoke.

When a nonsmoker breathes in secondhand smoke, he or she breathes in the four thousand or so harmful chemicals of the smoke. Carbon monoxide can cause fatigue and headaches. The chemicals can also cause lung disease and heart disease.

Many restaurant chains have started enacting smoke-free policies. These policies make it possible for nonsmokers to go out to eat without being trapped with dangerous secondhand smoke.

Studies have shown that nonsmokers who live with smokers die younger than people who live in smoke-free households.

What does all this mean? The nonsmoker who lives or works with smokers can get sick from the smoke just as smokers can. Is that fair? What do you think?

Protecting Nonsmokers

Let's say that you do not smoke. Think about riding in a car or being in a closed room with a smoker. The smoker's burning cigarette makes it hard for you to breathe. It may also drive you nuts because you know that the smoke is harming you. That is one of the reasons why antismoking laws exist across the country. These laws were designed to help and protect nonsmokers.

Today it is nearly impossible to smoke in public places in North America. Many state and local governments, as well as private companies, have imposed clean indoor air acts, or bans on smoking in places such as offices, restaurants, and stadiums. Public awareness about secondhand smoke and the dangers it poses for nonsmokers have made the bans acceptable and widespread.

And smoking isn't cheap, either! Just look at the price of cigarettes: in New York City, taxes in 2010 have increased the cost of one pack of cigarettes to $11 on average. A pack-a-day habit will cost you over $4,000 each year. Certainly you can think of better things to do with that money.

Smoking also limits your senses of taste and smell. Studies have shown that smoking gives you wrinkles and bad breath, and it makes your skin look unhealthy.

Part One: Reasons for Smoking	Very Important	Not Important
Smoking can make you feel like part of the group.	☐	☐
Smoking can make you feel more mature and glamorous.	☐	☐
If you already smoke, you would be giving up something that makes you feel good.	☐	☐
Smoking relaxes you.	☐	☐

Part Two: Reasons for Not Smoking	Very Important	Not Important
Smoking can limit your social life.	☐	☐
Smoking is bad for your health. It can even kill you.	☐	☐
It is bad for the health of others around you.	☐	☐
Smoking has special health risks for women.	☐	☐
Most public places prohibit smoking.	☐	☐
It reduces athletic ability.	☐	☐
It is an expensive habit.	☐	☐
Smoking makes your breath, clothes, and hair smell bad.	☐	☐

This Smoker's Decision Test is a good way for teens to understand why they are interested in smoking, as well as help them consider some of the consequences of choosing to smoke.

Making Up Your Mind About Smoking

Now you know more about smoking. You know how it affects your body, your appearance, and your health. You know more about why people start and why it is hard to stop.

Maybe you have not started smoking. Maybe your friends around you do, so you're considering it. Choosing whether to smoke is an important decision. The test on the facing page will help you. If you are already a smoker, try this test. It may change your mind about smoking.

The Smoker's Decision Test is not like a school test. There are no right or wrong answers. This is a way to help you get a clearer idea of what is important to you. It will help you make a decision about smoking. Copy the columns onto a piece of notebook paper or make a photocopy of the test in order to mark your answers. First, look closely at what you have checked in the Very Important column of Part One. Then proceed to Part Two.

Now write out your very important reasons for smoking and your very important reasons for not smoking. Compare them side-by-side.

Look at your reasons. Decide for yourself if you are going to start. If you have already started, decide if you are going to continue or quit. Either way, make your own decision.

Myths and Facts

 Myth **The younger you are when you start smoking, the easier it is to quit.** Fact The younger a person is when he starts smoking, the more likely he will develop a strong addiction to nicotine. Most young people who smoked regularly continue to smoke throughout adulthood.

 Myth **Smoking helps you lose weight.** Fact You may eat less if you smoke, but the weight gain you might experience when you quit (typically 10 to 15 pounds [4.5 to 6.8 kilograms]) is a smaller health hazard than smoking or using smokeless tobacco.

 Myth **The rate of teenage smoking keeps going up.** Fact The number of teenage smokers is actually decreasing. In fact, fewer teens ages fifteen to nineteen smoke now than in 2001.

HOW DO PEOPLE QUIT SMOKING?

Have you heard someone say that he or she is trying to quit smoking? This person has a real challenge ahead. Fortunately, the person is not alone, and there are several ways to get help. According to the NIH, more than thirty-five million people try to quit smoking each year. The CDC estimates that this is about 70 percent of all smokers. Teens—and even preteens—are a part of this group. According to a 2000 ALA study, the latest available data shows that more than 50 percent of middle school and high school smokers also tried to quit.

Smoking is a habit that is not easy to break. Many smokers wish that they had never started smoking. Perhaps they started because "everyone was doing it"

An important part of quitting is deciding when to do it, and then using willpower to stick to the decision. It is very difficult to overcome an addiction to nicotine, but deciding to quit is the first step.

or because they thought it would make them seem cool or more grown up. Perhaps they didn't know any better.

Most smokers have tried to quit, but many find that it is very hard. However, nearly half of all living adults who ever smoked have quit. That means there are millions of people who have quit smoking. Anybody can quit. There is no guaranteed method; each person has to find what is right for him or her. Here are some common steps to kicking the habit.

Making a List

Taking stock and making a list of all the reasons to quit is a great way for a smoker to motivate himself or herself to stop smoking. The reasons don't have to be complicated. For example:

- To feel in control of life
- To have better health
- To save money
- To protect family or friends from breathing second-hand smoke
- To feel free from addiction

A smoker can write down these reasons and keep the list handy every day. When the urge to smoke strikes, the smoker could pull out the list and read it, reminding himself or herself: this is why I'm quitting.

Setting a Date and Sticking to It

Another good tactic to quit is to choose a special date to quit and mark it on the calendar. Do not change it. If a smoker knows that he or she smokes most often at school or work, he or she should choose a weekend to quit. That will make the first one or two days easier.

There are two ways to quit that have worked for others. One is to quit gradually, smoking fewer and fewer cigarettes as the quitting date grows near. This forces the body to adjust to lower and lower nicotine levels. Another way is to quit cold turkey. Quitting cold turkey means that you choose the special day to quit, and you smoke until that day and never again. People who quit cold turkey don't use excuses; they use willpower to stay in the "I am done smoking forever" frame of mind.

Ways to Cut Down and Successfully Stop Smoking

Cutting down takes effort, but it is a good way to slowly adjust the body to the absence of nicotine. The trick to cutting down is monitoring smoking habits. Smokers often don't even think about the fact that they are smoking another cigarette. Some cigarettes, like the ones people smoke after a meal or a test, are more important. At those times the smoker really craves a cigarette. A smoker who is trying to cut down needs to decide which cigarette times are important and smoke only those cigarettes.

Another thing a smoker can do is plan ahead of time and carry the exact number of cigarettes that he or she has decided to smoke that day. It might be just two or three. Another way to cut down is to smoke only half a cigarette at a time. Smokers can also make cutting down easier by using a brand of cigarettes that they do not like. Icky-tasting cigarettes (ickier than the preferred brand) will help the smoker not want to reach for them so much. A smoker who wants to cut down should get rid of all his or her favorites and not buy new ones.

Still another way to cut down is to delay having a cigarette when the desire strikes. Instead of smoking when he wants to, the smoker waits ten minutes. That way he can think it over and decide if he really wants that cigarette. After ten minutes, he may not even want the cigarette anymore.

Changing the smoking routine works, too. Keeping cigarettes in a different place, smoking with the other hand, or even not doing anything else when smoking except thinking about how you feel while you are doing it are all good tactics.

Cutting down is great, but the smoker must not fool herself. She may think that she has things under control and that she can quit anytime. That is not true. Most people who cut down soon return to their original number of cigarettes.

Other Quitting Techniques

Telling family and friends about the plan to quit smoking can help. That will make it harder for the smoker to back out of it, and it will expand the smoker's support network. It will also let others know that the smoker might be cranky and a little hard to live with for a few days.

It's important that someone who is trying to quit smoking does not reach for a snack every time he or she wants a cigarette. Chewing gum and exercising are much better alternatives. Snacking on fatty foods or junk food could lead to weight gain. People often use weight gain as an excuse to start smoking again.

Finding other things to do that are fun or make you happy is crucial to cutting cigarettes out of your life. An easy choice is exercise. Exercise is good because you have to use your whole body. That reminds you of how important your lungs are. Also,

One effective strategy for quitting smoking is exercise. Playing sports is a good distraction from cravings and can also remind you how important a healthy, functioning body is.

exercise makes you feel good. Take up a hobby such as photography, music, or skateboarding. Go to the movies, the zoo, the beach, or a concert. To pay for these activities, use the money not being spent on cigarettes!

Hanging in There!

If a smoker caves and smokes a cigarette or even an entire pack, he should not feel that he has failed. He should pull out that list and remember why he is trying to quit. If the reasons have changed, the smoker should make a new list. When the urge to smoke arises, he should do something else instead and keep busy.

Smokers should watch for "smoke signals," like a friend lighting up. This is the time when someone who is trying to quit is most likely to smoke, but he or she must be strong and not give in to smoking. It will pay off.

Getting Help Quitting

Sometimes the smoker may believe that quitting cannot be done alone. It's OK to need help. There are millions of people who have had to ask for help. Smokers should be proud of themselves for realizing their own limitations and understanding that they need help. The good news is getting help is easy. Many organizations are out there to help.

Teenage smokers can check with teachers, guidance counselors, or school nurses to find out if their school offers a program

Nicotine gum is a helpful tool for someone who is trying to quit smoking. The gum releases a small amount of nicotine to satisfy the smoker's cravings without the tar and smoke that come with smoking a cigarette.

to help students kick the habit. If the school does not have such a program, counselors should be able to help find a program.

There are many organizations to help smokers kick the habit, such as the American Cancer Society, the American Lung Association, and the Foundation for a Smoke-Free America. All three have programs to educate the public and help smokers. For information on contacting these organizations, check out the For More Information section of this book.

Help can come from several sources. Doctors can prescribe medicine to help break the addiction. Some people succeed in quitting smoking by using special chewing gum. Others find help by using a nicotine patch, which is a small pad (similar to a bandage) that, when placed on your body, releases small amounts of nicotine into your skin. It gives your body the nicotine it craves without all the other harmful chemicals in a cigarette. Both the gum and the patch can help steer the body away from nicotine.

When trying to quit, one may find it helpful to get some counseling. Deciding to quit smoking is a major step and can create feelings of stress, unhappiness, and irritability. There are many changing emotions to cope with in addition to coping with fighting nicotine cravings. And sometimes it helps to have someone to talk to, who will listen to you and offer you the support needed.

Conclusion

Now that you have learned some of the facts, do you still think smoking sounds cool? Is smoking really worth the damage that it will cause your body? Deciding whether to smoke is your choice. While making that choice, be aware of the perils involved. You have learned about the health risks associated with smoking, as well as how smoking can affect your social life. If you are still curious about smoking, get all the facts before you take that first puff from a cigarette, cigar, or pipe. Smoking is a dead end—literally—so deciding to smoke is not a casual choice. Make this important decision while respecting yourself. You are important and you deserve good health. If you are already addicted and you want to quit smoking, remember that there are people and organizations that can help you on the road to recovery. You've made a great choice for better health, and you deserve a smoke-free, nicotine-free life.

Glossary

addiction A condition in which a person's body depends on a habit-forming chemical or substance.

adrenal gland A gland that produces the hormone adrenaline. Adrenaline prepares the body for emergency action; it makes the heart work harder.

bronchi Tubes in the lungs.

bronchitis A condition marked by severe coughing and irritation of the lungs that is often caused by smoking.

cancer A disease that causes cells to grow abnormally and become tumors. These tumors spread and interfere with normal cell growth.

carbon dioxide A gas that is poisonous. It is one of the chemicals in cigarette smoke.

carbon monoxide A gas that is breathed out of the body during exhalation.

cilia Tiny hairs in the bronchi that clear away mucus.

craving A great desire or longing.

drag The inhalation of cigarette smoke.

emphysema A condition marked by severe coughing and irritation of the lungs that is often caused by smoking.

heart disease One of a number of health problems such as heart attack, stroke, hardening of the arteries, and blood clots.

influence To sway or affect.

lung cancer A disease in which the cells of the lungs divide uncontrollably. Smoking is a major cause of lung cancer.

mainstream smoke What a smoker inhales and exhales.

mucus A slippery secretion that coats and protects mucous membranes.

nicotine A drug found in tobacco to which your body becomes addicted.

peer pressure The feeling of being compelled by someone in your social group to do things that you might not do on your own.

premature Early; before being fully ready.

sidestream smoke The smoke that comes from the burning end of a cigarette.

stress Tension or pressure.

tar A sticky black substance found in tobacco. It coats the lungs when smoke is inhaled.

withdrawal The process of stopping the body's dependency on an addictive drug; the physical and mental effects an addict suffers after ceasing to take an addictive drug.

Action on Smoking and Health (ASH)
2013 H Street NW
Washington, DC 20006
(202) 659-4310
Web site: http://www.ash.org
Founded in 1967, ASH is a nonprofit, scientific, and educational organization that has been lobbying for
nonsmokers' rights on a federal level. ASH supported
the legislation that banned cigarette advertising on television and currently fights for indoor smoking bans in
public places, among many other goals to protect the
health of nonsmokers.

American Cancer Society (ACS)
1599 Clifton Road
Atlanta, GA 30329
(800) ACS-2345 (227-2345)
Web site: http://www.cancer.org
ACS can provide information on smoking-related cancers.

American Lung Association
61 Broadway, 6th Floor
New York, NY 10006
Web site: http://www.lungusa.org

Find the latest research and information about lung disease, including smoking-related disease, treatment, and resources for quitting smoking.

Canadian Cancer Society
Suite 200, 10 Alcorn Avenue
Toronto, ON M4V 3B1
Canada
(416) 961-7223
Web site: http://www.cancer.ca
The Canadian Cancer Society is a national, community-based organization of volunteers whose mission is the eradication of cancer and the enhancement of the quality of life of people living with cancer.

Foundation for a Smoke-Free America
8117 Manchester Avenue, Suite 500
Playa del Rey, CA 90293
(310) 577-9828
Web site: http://www.anti-smoking.org
The Foundation for a Smoke-Free America strives to keep young people tobacco-free and works to empower and motivate smokers to quit through a variety of educational programs in communities and schools across the country.

The Lung Association
1750 Courtwood Crescent, Suite 300
Ottawa, ON K2C 2B5

Canada

(613) 569-6411

Web site: http://www.lung.ca

The Lung Association has a mission of promoting and improv-
ing lung health for all Canadians.

Web Sites

Due to the changing nature of Internet links, Rosen Publishing
has developed an online list of Web sites related to the subject
of this book. This site is updated regularly. Please use this link
to access the list:

http://www.rosenlinks.com/faq/smo

Bellenir, Karen, ed. *Tobacco Information for Teens: Health Tips About the Hazards of Using Cigarettes, Smokeless Tobacco, and Other Nicotine*. Detroit, MI: Omnigraphics, 2010.

Bjornlund, Lydia. *Teen Smoking*. San Diego, CA: ReferencePoint Press, 2009.

Connolly, Sean. *Tobacco*. North Mankato, MN: Smart Apple Media, 2007.

Evans, Lesli B. *But All My Friends Smoke!: Cigarettes and Peer Pressure*. Broomall, PA: Mason Crest Publishers, 2009.

Hansen, Julia. *A Life in Smoke: A Memoir*. New York, NY: Free Press, 2006.

Herrick, Charles, Charlotte Herrick, and Marianne Mitchell. *100 Questions and Answers About How to Quit Smoking*. Sudbury, MA: Jones and Bartlett Publishers, 2010.

Hudson, David L. *Smoking Bans*. New York, NY: Chelsea House Publishers, 2008.

Hyde, Margaret O., and John F. Setaro. *Smoking 101: An Overview for Teens*. Minneapolis, MN: Twenty-First Century Books. 2006.

Malaspina, Ann. *False Images, Deadly Promises: Smoking and the Media*. Broomall, PA: Mason Crest Publishers, 2009.

McKay, William, and Heath Dingwell. *The Truth About Smoking*. New York, NY: Facts On File, 2009.

Meinking, Mary. *Cash Crop to Cash Cow: The History of Tobacco and Smoking in America*. Philadelphia, PA: Mason Crest Publishers, 2009.

Porterfield, Jason. *Tobacco*. New York, NY: Rosen Publishing Group, 2008.

Rabinoff, Michael. *Ending the Tobacco Holocaust: How Big Tobacco Affects Our Health, Pocketbook, and Political Freedom and What We Can Do About It*. Santa Rosa, CA: Elite Books, 2010.

Sharp, Katie John. *Smokeless Tobacco: Not a Safe Alternative*. Broomall, PA: Mason Crest Publishers, 2009.

Thomas, Amy. *Burning Money: The Cost of Smoking*. Broomall, PA: Mason Crest Publishers, 2009.

Williams, Roger, ed. *Teen Smoking*. Detroit, MI: Greenhaven Press, 2009.

Index

A

adrenal glands, 31–32
adrenaline, 32
alcohol, 15, 28
American Cancer Society
    (ACS), 4, 12, 19, 53
American Heart Association
    (AHA), 12
American Lung Association
    (ALA), 6, 8, 22, 25, 45, 53
antismoking laws, 41
association, 8
asthma, 35

B

bad breath, 16, 36, 41
bans, 8, 41
birth control pills, 25
breast cancer, 25
bronchitis, 24, 27

C

Camel, Joe, 10
Camel No. 9 cigarettes, 10
cancer, 16, 18, 19, 24, 25, 32, 38
carbon monoxide, 20, 39
Centers for Disease Control
    and Prevention (CDC),
    4, 45
chewing gum, 49, 53
cigars, 54
cold turkey, quitting, 48

contests, 12
Cosmopolitan, 10
crack cocaine, 15, 28

E

emphysema, 24
environmental tobacco
    smoke, 38
exercise, 25, 49, 51

F

Flintstone, Fred, 10
Foundation for a Smoke-Free
    America, 53

H

heart attacks, 25, 27
heart disease, 16, 18, 20, 32, 39
heroin, 28

I

infertility, 16

J

*Journal of the American
    Medical Association*, 10

L

Lorillard Tobacco Company, 12
Lung Association, 6, 22, 39
lung cancer, 16, 18, 19, 25,
    32, 38

About the Authors

Veronica Stollers is a writer and nonsmoker living and breathing easily in Eugene, Oregon.

Elizabeth Keyishian is a writer living in New York City.

Photo Credits

Cover Ian Hooton/SPL/Getty Images; p. 5 Adam Gault/ Digital Vision/Getty Images; p. 9 MCT/Landov; p. 11 Roger L. Wollenberg/UPI/Landov; p. 14 Alex Wong/Getty Images; p. 17 Garry Hunter/Photographer's Choice/Getty Images; p. 21 iStockphoto/Thinkstock; p. 23 CMSP/J. L. Carson/Collection Mix: Subjects/Getty Images; p. 26 from Proposed Cigarette Product Warning Labels at http://www.fda.gov/TobaccoProducts/ Labeling/CigaretteProductWarningLabels/default.htm; p. 30 © www.istockphoto.com/Martin McCarthy; p. 31 Dr. Arthur Tucker/Photo Researchers, Inc.; p. 37 Graeme Robertson/Getty Images; pp. 39, 40 Tim Boyle/Getty Images; p. 46 Peter Dazeley/ Photographer's Choice/Getty Images; p. 50 Photodisc/Thinkstock; p. 52 Steve Horrell/SPL/Getty Images.

Designer: Evelyn Horovicz; Photo Researcher: Karen Huang